LATE IN THE ANTENNA FIELDS

FUTUREPOEM BOOKS

2011

LATE IN THE

ANTENNA

FIELDS

Alan Gilbert

FIRST EDITION | FIRST PRINTING

This edition first published in paperback by Futurepoem books
P.O. Box 7687 JAF Station, NY, NY 10116
www.futurepoem.com

Executive Editor: Dan Machlin
Editor/Production: Chris Martin

Cover design: Mickel Design (www.mickeldesign.com)
Cover image: Paul Chan, *1st Light*, 2005. Digital video projection. 14 minutes. Courtesy
the artist and Greene Naftali Gallery.
Photograph by Louise Wright © 2009 under the Creative Commons license
Typesetting: Mary Austin Speaker (www.maryaustinspeaker.com)
Typefaces: Superior-Light (Cover); Bruce Old Style (Text)

Printed in the United States of America on acid-free paper

State of the Arts

NYSCA

Futurepoem is supported in part by a grant from the New York State Council
on the Arts, a state agency, as well as by individual donors and subscribers.
Additional marketing support for this book was provided by The Creative Capital
Foundation. Futurepoem books is the publishing program of Futurepoem, Inc.,
a New York State-based 501(c)3 non-profit organization dedicated to creating a
greater public awareness and appreciation of innovative literature.

Distributed to the trade by Small Press Distribution, Berkeley, California
Toll-free number (U.S. only): 800.869.7553
Bay Area/International: 510.524.1668
orders@spdbooks.org
www.spdbooks.org

ACKNOWLEDGMENTS

Versions of some of these poems first appeared in the following publications: *Big Bridge*, BOMB, *Boston Review, Canarium, Damn the Caesars, Denver Quarterly, Hot Whiskey, jubilat, The Nation, Tarpaulin Sky,* and *Thuggery & Grace*. Many thanks to their respective editors.

"The consolation for proper behavior is" was published as a broadside to accompany the exhibition *Springtide*, held at the Institute of Contemporary Art, Philadelphia.

Particular thanks to the whole Futurepoem crew—including Dan Machlin, Jeremy Sigler, Mónica de la Torre, Jay Sanders, Chris Martin, and Mary Austin Speaker—for making this book possible. Thanks also to Paul Chan, Greene Naftali Gallery, and cover designer Jeremy Mickel. Grateful acknowledgment is made to Creative Capital for its generous support of this project.

CONTENTS

SIGNAL CALLERS MEET THE WAVE MACHINE

FOR FUTURE TRIPS OR EVERYDAY LIFE

COMMERCE

CITY

VISTAS

THE WORLD ONE SUMMER

The day was still but the animals were moving.
We took a number and stood in line.
Sometimes the wounded land softly and sometimes with a thud.
Holes in the roof shine like stars.

A cake sat out on the counter for too long.
We were pinched between big machines.
A fleet of cargo ships stretches from the harbor to the sea.
The city's walls keep me company.

Give the Grammy to the sampler; it earned it.
My daughter fixes the sun to the sky.
It's frequently a bore to hear people narrate their dreams.
Small scars around the eyes map hunger and distraction.

That's how the dining experience came to be called splatter.
You said it all felt very post-disco.
Sitcoms are funnier without any sound.
But in the quiet of the night I occasionally hear weeping.

OUTPATIENT PROCEDURE

The dawn would be nice if it didn't arrive so early.
      I don't know why I rarely want what I can have.
There's a logic to animals and to tumbleweed assembly lines
      reconfigured between shifts to produce Escalade interiors.
But it doesn't quench my addiction to you, as a family
      of civilian ghosts phase-shifts through the fog lights
      piercing an Olive Garden parking lot.

Switch the camera over to movie mode. My favorite
      bartender storyboarded the decline of the rural gentry
while clearing away the empties. The remaining spills
      dribble uphill at $100 a barrel, like buying a whole CD
to hear one love song or renting a lifeboat by the hour
      in the Arctic. I used to be the person in my building
      who dragged the trash curbside each week.

A hand moves across the sky. I already said that I've made
      mistakes, though they don't include spot-ironing wrinkles
out of the matches stored next to the kerosene and feeding strays
      with the other neighborhood housewives while performing
the rain dance. I fade just a little bit when your star goes away.
      It could be midnight madness in the middle of the day
      and still remain quiet.

But these used hospital slippers fit the system or the individual
       watching dirty bathwater swirl down the drain. There goes
our safe space, ignoring a knock at the door. Children don't give up
       on love and say where will the snow carry you?
After 9/11, I felt frozen in place and didn't leave the city
       for almost a year. Then the police came to take
       away the pain.

POEM WITHOUT A CODA

The music ended before the band stopped
playing, as we pantomime our quiet disappointments
with a smile sifting the years through sharpened
metal colanders, asking, If it's organic, does that
mean we can eat it? Planes

                and blimps fly low over
the house to avoid spacecraft preparing a global
holiday light show featuring famous U.S. presidents
enjoying Coca-Cola snow cones, cued to the sky
fading from slate blue to black.

If being infatuated with the idea of tube
socks but not actual tube socks makes me a dreamer,
then I'll take three pairs to go, because I'm only
in this for the money and complimentary hors d'oeuvres
incorporating gag reflex

              suppressants, as angels
and insects crawl on my face, tracing their own
partially haphazard flights of desire, their digitally
altered exit wounds scratching a scanner's polished
surface.

Each day we try to do a little bit better,
and mostly end up staying the same. Each day we look
for something other than what's been taken away.

It's destruction that compels us to destroy while
cherishing big top fantasies

                             of mortars bouncing off
the circus tent as the ringmaster's wireless mic
gleams with popcorn butter and massage oil—
whatever it takes to keep initiation rituals hidden
behind a lace curtain patched with a satisfying read.

       I don't know how I lived so long without
you, and yet I still don't live with you, so let
the honeysuckles take all the dew. For better
and for worse, bodies are permeable structures,
but what gets in cells

                           has trouble getting out.
Paper hangers twist with clothes wet enough
to collect sediment on walking tours of what
remains unspoken; otherwise, wax the astronaut's
lifejacket cords for flossing after splashdown.

       It's called home-for-now; then it spills
over into what looks like tomorrow, with its
bandana worn over the neck, mouth, or hair.
Sometimes I just sit there and stare. Language
floods the gaps and jingles

                      the hedges, leaving
watermarks around the gravediggers' wrists

bound with cellophaned variety packs while
foraging sex's dumpster. The prettiest calendars
are made from dryer lint in gradual dispersion.

When the electric garage door opened,
the teenage punks tumbled out with their squirrel
guns. I hung back with the plastic trash cans.
A product recall press conference was like a quiz
show in which contestants

had to guess the wrong
answers: grey flags, donkey filets, age spots, and
Dewar's. Thankfully, there was a potato and set
of false teeth in the refrigerator. Please warm
before inserting.

ANYTHING EXCEPT CHARMING

The only naps I take are in the morning
after a night spent choking on stars.
Sometimes people go missing;
other times it's me.
Still, it's a lonely life for being so crowded,
or else it takes a club member
to get you in.
Each backyard or nearby field
contained a small oil well guarded
by a dingo wearing lopsided bunny ears.
Inside, you can hear the sound of crickets chirping,
as talk show hosts interview hospice workers.

On the table is a box of disposable gloves
used to serve cafeteria food.
Deckhands dodge a wildly swaying mainsail
while paralyzed from the neck up
after long days at the office
stacking wooden pallets.
In archery class,
I badly overshot every target,
and generally stumbled onto the ecstatic,
just as it's anything except charming to answer
the door naked and waving a piece of bacon.

not manners, but one ventricle filled with spiders,
    the other with M&M's. Getting dressed
for the office is a contortionist's act when the body
    is skin's coat rack for however long
you can endure it. Repeat daily while resting a plate
    on your head, as epaulets collect dust
under the sofa of a distant home, with clouds specially
    flown in for the occasion. After the blizzard,
the obsessives challenged the compulsives to a game
    of snowflake removal. I'm still coming
undone, even though TV has taught me how to live again.

Love is another issue altogether. It refuses to stay
    fixed with hairspray, and may feel
a little bit painful. And playful—like Orpheus eating
    a hot dog. Better that than the egg
salad sandwich rotisseried in the hot afternoon sun.
    Newspapers label it Arts and Leisure;
we call it downwind from the prosthetics factory.
    Every performance implies a spotlight,
even if it means driving through the night to get there,
    mouth wired open in a grimace
or grin. Memories send back their half-candid blessings.

It's no fun being sick in a strange country. Movie
    audiences never saw the violence
of back rooms. The fact that it was springtime didn't
    make it any easier, all the crutches
and arm slings covered in jasmine and nettles crashing
    through the plastic orange cones.
I'd wave and nod approvingly, but it might rumple
    the thin pink saliva necktie connecting
my chin to my shoes. The wishing well is under constant
    surveillance projected or internal.
Mirrors are not the same and are messier than they look.

                            —*after Patty Chang*

HEALING HEARTS THROUGH THE ARTS

I.

We built the pyramids in a weekend
        and imported roses.
The renovations will never be finished.
An eel wrapped its way up 20-lb. test line
              after the hook got snagged
       on the gunboats' reflections.
The oceans are filled with sharks.
Instinct is its own form of expectation,
        subsisting partly on fear.
But that's not why our makeup runs in streaks.
It's because we're still hungry.
It's because no amount of language will fill this space,
          and the closer you get the farther it moves away—
             the inverse proportion to saying yes
              and silent afternoons;
moreover, my passport photo barely resembles me.
I fought against the king while Sophie dreamed
       of princesses dancing.
In the morning,
we found ourselves alone again,
        sunshine slowly spilling through the room,
as seagulls drift among the lines randomly
       dividing land from water.

II.

Loose cannons roll across the deck of a pirate ship
        during its confrontation with an automated
                wave machine,
while down below
the crew plays online shuffleboard
        against retirees in Florida.
Crates of pears rot a day's drive from a famine trading
        zebra heads for gold.
I'm mostly okay with the verbs and objects,
        less so with the subjects,
like waiting patiently to deliver a child—
        an infrared gardener with a license
                to fail.
The factories are open all night,
        missing causes for the effects turned into
what-can-we-get-away-with?
                                such as
        leaning our faces to the dust,
                pressing our hands to the light,
                        and plugging our ears to the winners.
Replant the trees in spring.
Even the bowl is edible,
                the air full of static,
        during decades spent on the stand.
The extra chair is for pneumonia.
It's hard to keep the cold cream jar clean
or the prom clear of underage drinkers.

III.

Downtime to the downtime is known as death
or ingesting excessive mercury levels,

                                        I forget,

while spinning in a homemade hammock
           strung in front of a TV.
His family owns a house in the country.
I got the directions confused.
Doing the dishes can be relaxing
           after serving microwave parts for dinner
once the cupboards are bare except for
           cumulative dust and collapsing stars.
It's the state versus roughing art up,
           along with tender
                      and sometimes overcome with grief.
Floodwaters float us and the plastic toys in the bathtub.
These aren't the brand of staples that fasten
           flesh to flesh;
they don't secure our lives to hope,
           just letters to their corners like blindspots
               to the passing lane.
Local officials stagger the hunting season
               as the town turns out in orange and camouflage,
           then checks the weather report.
I see deer by the side of the road.
Bad year expected for mountain wildflowers.

IV.

Heretics are rarely caught cooking outdoors with loss
        tattooed to their wrists.
It's not just an organ transplant
                                but the whole human.
What's the point in memorializing the ongoing,
        even with these aortas left over and mapped
as far as neurons stumbling around before dawn
in someone else's bathrobe labeled
        lithium,
                cotton/synthetic fibers,
                        and satellite radio?
Love can be dark in what it touches.
Love makes us better in the end.
Squeeze the neck of the mandolin
        while cradling its body.
Workers anticipate another round of layoffs
        after the construction of Sparta.
The law of the father hurls a ham in a wind tunnel
        and runs wet fingers through its hair.
Cells briefly contract with each
                        separation,
as the halfway house gets emptied out for a new paint job.
Residents grabbed bracelets and air filters
        clogged with debris,
leaving panhandlers to sift through the backyard's
        compost heap
visited by fireflies
                with tiny flashlights
        clustering in temporary constellations.

FIRST BRING THE LOVE THEN BRING THE NOISE

Autobiography is a soup
is today's favored dentures
soaked while sitting
on a thin branch struck
against the light as a cloud
of dust rises in outer space
and randomly scatters
while I chase each piece
with a crooked rake then
lean against the stainless
steel seating sloped
like an ear's cartilage
for sweeping in corners

A dog barks at ghosts
before they turn into people
we see the people turn
into ghosts or TV hijacking
a scrambled alphabet
of desire a to b it doesn't
always have to rhyme
what was left of the digging
was done with plastic spoons
and frequent underwear
changes filling the suggestion
box with Dear Santa
I promise I've been good

this year except for that
incident with the pork chop
at the tanning salon

After all that how did I
end up staring at the same
wall again first bring
the love then bring the noise
past the language of supermarket
shelves mixed in a Google
spittoon and smelling like
a global-style sunscreen
tossing live grenades
or handfuls of trail mix
over a volleyball net used
by boys with their rings
not of fire but of bruises
brushing low-slung bikes
rusting in orchards

Forget what I just said
history is unbecoming
in the perpetual present's
torches and pitchforks
surrounding a house and its
enamel-on-metal kicked-over
going-out-of-business sign
I got used to the disappointment
but what I still hate

is being ordered around
so I wear the same suit
to weddings job interviews
and funerals with a hammer
in the jacket pocket
and a soft-necked vase
for all the flowers given

like consolation-prize
perfume because the machines
are us but not ours the days
are ours but not us staining
commuter-line schedules
with used napkins or stuffing
appetites the imagination
trips over while stepping out
of the shower as a purple
bathrobe with a ragged hem
drags its belt behind it
the conditions of exile
are unique to each home lost
slowly or without warning

HOME
ON THE
STRANGE

COOLANT SYSTEM

It's not heroic, it's broken. It's the silent trip
between unspokens. We recognize the architecture
but don't name it. We take a place amid the holes
resembling pink dots inside our fathers' hearts.
All the little words don't even reach the doorbell.

Some people are awake in the middle of the night.
Some are at the bathroom sink rinsing and spitting.
There's a PowerPoint presentation for just about
anything, and a personalized ringtone to alert us
when the war is calling—it's the sound of beds
being dragged across an orphanage floor.

The next ice age will fill the rivers with antifreeze.
It's the midway point of a sugar packet's half-life,
spoonfed in timelapse with porn made to order.
I still briefly pause when I hear an airplane flying
low. The police helicopters I'm more used to,
as an ebbing river of concrete reveals a beach
strewn with Mardi Gras necklaces hurled
at the Superdome.

We change the sheets for the next set of guests.
We live with contradictions. At a benefit
for eating off plasma TVs, my gift bag contained
a woman's razor and chocolate-covered pretzels;
yours was filled with Play-Doh and a snorkel.

Initial programming includes episodes of *Pimp My Ride*
for self-propelled cyborgs randomly chosen
for modifications after fending off drunks swinging
gravy ladles.

Donkeys do well in semi-arid desert. Manny or
Mandy? Who will heal the healers? Someone
smeared a label warning Do Not Ingest. Clouds
move quickly ahead of the front and a rush to close
the windows. Normally, I'd say it was a good thing
we were home, where worn-out shoes are left curbside
with the other paper and plastic recycling.

EVERY 20-GALLON JAR OF PICKLES CONTAINS A FREE

totem pole and a collectable holographic

trading card featuring a different street battle
in Iraq seen through green vinegar and beer.

Emergency lights flashed in the forest
as the state trooper stiffly asked for license

and registration; I tried to act casual while
swallowing time, since it was the only

relevant piece of evidence. Please believe
me when I say I've been bowing, though

perhaps I haven't been bowing low
enough. Before the photojournalists

arrived, the craters were bombed to make
bigger craters breaking every narrative

into messy topographies and fault lines.
A newsboy hawks the evening edition

with its story about ducks on frayed couches
skimming their meal from the surface

of darkened information and spilled meaning.
You aren't even the masters of your own

wars, your teeth chattering against the TV
screen, like a seeing-eye monkey with a

porn addiction squinting at the flickering
pictures. Too much is an advertisement

for more. We only heard the trains late
at night while dreaming of hobos, our bellies

stuffed with Lean Cuisine. The side of corn
showed up in our stools at the top hat,

while wrinkles in the wallpaper turned out
to be missing Cheerios and roach traps

linked by thick trails of sugar. That was before
a bee got into my alphabet. Horses with shiny

hindquarters in transcontinental quarantine
watch polo players scatter from runways

when the cargo planes approach after having
emptied their payloads of cluster bombs,

Snickers bars, and flat-tire repair kits
on the women and children first. A drunk

visiting poet took a rowboat and the reception's
last bottle of wine onto a fog-bound lake.

During group therapy, I roleplayed a thumb
washer to the dental hygienist. The day

is quiet for remembering and then forgetting
again, the quick flash of history and medical

tests, because writing is solitary in execution
and collective in everything else, a second-level

listening making slow drips glimmer.

I THINK IT WOULD BE BETTER IF I DIDN'T SING

Dusk slips into the car, fastens its seat belt,
and rests a toiletry bag on its knees where
the day skews toward later and its windfall
of neglect, its magazines stuffed in the garbage.

To the fish's cloudy-eyed constituency,
it wasn't international surrealism but a wave
curling a knife to its handle. And while
it's true we could try to wrestle the banana

away from that formidable gorilla, wouldn't it
be better to reason with it first, and if that fails,
to try to confuse it with Mel Tormé's screen test
for *Planet of the Apes*? Or have I disappointed

you again by nodding off in church? Besides,
I need to check my email and various online
meat retailers selling dehydrated beef suppositories
dunked in a saucer of milk as antibiotics climb

the blood's bowl within the silence of no.
In other words, a smooth exit was derailed
when my sleeve snagged on a nail jutting from
an inexpensive rosé my parents swear by.

LEASE TO OWN

Termites barely left enough for kindling,
then retreated to the recliner's metal springs
while aerial bombers bounce off the headrest.

We lace our fingers in a chain-link fence
to get a better view of the cockpit's back row
of navigators whiting out their pupils.

Only the humans lie on *Wild Kingdom,*
especially while shaving with a straight
razor. Art gives the right of first refusal.

Still, we'll follow whatever haunts you,
so go ahead and finish that meal.
There's the fear of drowning but not of dying,

as dust slowly sinks through the diagonal light.
It doesn't really matter what I do when
I'm alone and sanding down the drywall.

The oceans hardened into crystals. Starfish
armed themselves for the evening's slideshow
of plastic bags tumbling in the Gulf Stream.

The device was already damaged, so we
upgraded the battery instead, watching
hobbled animals outrun the vultures

and feeling restless where we live. The café
was sold out of our favorite doughnuts,
though that doesn't excuse kicking over

artificial plants in a doctor's office where
history archives itself with assorted syringes.
I'm not sure what to do when the steering wheel

shakes loose. The pizza delivery guy
and orchard keeper swapped t-shirts behind
the gas station. What's an errand, anyway?

There's a rhythm to the hills accompanied
by the right air-conditioned soundtrack
blurring the landscape in clouds of exhaust.

Date stamps press light or heavy, scraping
a little bit of everything from under the nails.
But I set fire to that boat a long time ago.

NOT OR BUT AND

Speed reading keeps the fact-checkers busy while sifting
      through piles of lick-'em-and-stick-'em, glow-in-the-dark
stars that then get jammed in the printer, rushing right past
      the sentimental to reach the tragic, because playing nice
is much harder than being nice, so I tuck my pant legs
      into my socks to keep the wind and rain off at the higher
velocities, the simple yet fundamental mass-to-propulsion
      ratio, the simultaneous impact of recuperation and letting go.

A poet in this culture puts everything in the mouth, which
      isn't the same as all-you-can-eat, whether dining communally
or alone if the meds are interacting correctly and the paycheck
      hasn't already been spent on a shopping-channel exclusive
desktop sonar unit bouncing sound waves off the underwater-
      mine-detecting dolphins' fake-nose-and-moustache disguise
worn to the test for identifying proper names, I call: Here come
      the bosses—look busy!

The extensive renovations next door dislodge the roaches
      and mice but not every Tuesday night's PTA meeting concerns
in the fragile ecotone you tried to show me as I wondered
      if the car's heater would even work this winter from stuffing
the vents with emergency provisions for the long drive home
      to the glue-factory warehouse with its brand of forgetting,
unless, perhaps, it's the slowly starving, search-and-destroy
      approach to food preparation and cruise-ship-waste dumping.

There were some feeble attempts to make a pile out of whatever
        mixed-up form loss and desire shape, as you dream of reaching
up to adjust a façade like an oversized pair of sunglasses
        resting crooked against your face after a partially documented
fender-bender with a wayward paparazzi got blogged about
        in an online police blotter before watching the *Daily Show* and
Adult Swim, the microwavable nachos' fluorescent yellow
        cheese sauce dripping on our jeans.

That's when you leaned in and said, Let's find a way to heal,
        to no one in particular, and the clouds floated backward
without rewinding time, because all categories are fabrications,
        one side drops bombs the other brings down airplanes, and my arm
briefly went numb from the inoculation, although I wasn't feeling
        desperate yet, just outpriced by a neighborhood I moved into
on the heels of someone else's broken marriage, but first
        the nurse warned, This is probably going to hurt a little.

PILLOW TALK

Dating is like a mouthwash siphon.
>The literal needs setting up.

Never in a million years is still a relative amount.
>I can't say that just because it looks cheap, it isn't.

There are people who will teach you not to love unconditionally,
>and that can be the hardest lesson of all.

But most categories are bogus.
>In my quietest moments I think of you.

Marine snow drifts softly through the saline dark.
>Air travel carves grooves in the ozone.

After all the handicapped spaces were taken,
>the only spot left was next to a fire hydrant.

I monogrammed the hand towels used for plugging-up leaks
>in the slaughterhouse ceiling.

Language outruns its object when it doesn't scab over,
>occupying more worlds than one.

Massage directly into the skin or inject
>with small needles wobbling at their pivot.

I agree, almost everything sucked
>about tonight's made-for-TV movie.

GO SOLAR

Cartoon characters don't age, they get canceled.
A lifeguard missed the shark attack while reading
the articles of impeachment. After years of enduring
such a fucked-up situation, the question of blame
became relative, and longevity gets more difficult
to spell. Is the context going to be love, the impossible
imagination of mourning quickly?

Some of my best friends are machines tracing dust
back to the body, the night to the sun searing
a massive oil spill scooped from backyard swimming
pools with spatulas and patched with hair dryers
applying decals advertising the local speakeasy
serving a rubbed-off shine backed by a bucketful
of teeth.

Gargoyles decorate a gothic dollhouse balustrade
after being banished from the playground, so if
the penguins want to have a good time in their
sequel, I'm not going to hold it against either them
or my petty-drug-dealing neighbor tending his rooftop
garden and pit bulls while we embrace the constraints
soaking a cardboard shelter.

When will I see you again? Rats invading igloos
means it's time to go solar or dye chlorophyll orange.
I don't know exactly where the money will come from.

All the drinking water was diverted to the golfcourse
greens, yet the dream remains alive of someday
stocking our own terrarium with nerve damage,
late bloomers, and a senate's quicksand bandwagon.

Which is to say, I'm kinda hopeful hearing the wind
in those dwarf spruce trees that don't seem quite as tall
now that we're older. Hail to the Thermo King, because
maybe we just need to learn to chill out a little
instead of always outguessing the morning's muffin
selection, of losing the thread in the everyday cubicle's
managed swamp gas.

Meanwhile, children run right into the nets tossed
at delivery trucks and strays. Narrative tucks information
in. So how would you explain the opaque quartz
animal leaning into me? Or the silk gloves for each fist
on the oars jabbing elevator buttons? Or a hand pressed
to a red electric burner? Each of the calendar's months
pictures a different prison neck tattoo.

What's the romance in getting lost at sea? Most boats
rarely pass beyond the city's skyline. Images are translated
into numbers, even the drunk elephant jiggling on screen.
The next day the rulers were slaves building corn syrup
clocks ticking off addiction's economy of desire and
resurfacing symptoms dragging their scaly tails across
dinner plates.

A ceiling fan wobbles in its mount above a light breeze
rolling low off the water. A screened-in-porch protects
paper plates and fishing bait, as the heat stretches
out mouths and makes the *plastique* unstable. Give
and move on is what our mothers told us when they
were sick. Then learn to sit patiently in a room filled
with voices, with every viral promissory note.

SPITTING IMAGE

All the toxic runoff
drained into a green pond
behind the house
where the you-said/I-said
tire swing slowly
pulls loose from
its timber moorings
while it's nighttime
with the windows open
in any kind of weather
eroding skeletons
pushing up through
carpets and tack strips,
because love is what
undoes us.

I'm a collection
of flesh and implants
dropped in the mail
each day to the hummed
Miss America pageant
theme song,
like an army pack
that weighs more
than the soldier,
so this time I'll try it
without breathing

and the parents who
see their imagination
of you, deftly directing
rubber-tipped crutches
over scattered handfuls
of sand and rock salt.

Light is the first thing
lost, the clipped speech
of forgetting in the present,
as a detached astronaut
silently floats out
of radio transmission
range, just as most
of the brain's capacities
are taken up with
bodily functions,
including the ongoing
generation of scar tissue
and eyelids twitching
from gas station fumes.

We saw big casinos
replaced by bigger
casinos using the extra
gaming table felt
to make a bonnet
for Celine Dion's baby
and floral centerpieces

that resemble insects,
even though on cold days
it feels good to have
a stomach filled with
toy helicopters piled
against a garage storing
disassembled floats for
the homecoming parade.

Even the fed grew lean on the carvings
      served up by tomorrow.
Only the owner is allowed to beat his dogs.
Luckily,
we were chewing mouthfuls of rubber bands
      when the car scraped the guardrail.
I glanced back while awaiting the next message.
The law sleeps on the symbolic;
                      it lifts our prints,
like the sirens that wake us up early on Sundays.
Hollywood is sincere,
but I'm with Cam'ron when it comes to wearing
man sandals
      in the Hamptons.

Everyone seemed so friendly at the porn awards show,
with free valet parking for our car.
The sky looks too far away.
Then it peeked above the mirror
      behind the bar.
That's why I was grateful to have met you
      while doing laundry and waving at the dead.
You make the darkness all aglitter
      at midnight bowling for dollars with disco balls.
The important information fit on a laptop,
except for a history of repair worn loosely
      as a beauty pageant sash
            to the gas station.

To want what you can't have is
     75% disappointment
     and 25% mysticism,
or a labyrinth instead of the thread.

Nevertheless,
we picked you since you're the least likely
     to embarrass us,
               especially now
that I'm wearing an Aquaman costume to the mall.
Next door
       is a house with a kid and a small yard but no father.
It was the last place we lived
          where we left
     the front door unlocked.
Breakdancing troupes make a tour of rural schools
     after classes on how to read contrails
     and military enlistments.
The block party is slow in getting started.
We're still awaiting the forecaster's rain.

ECHO POETICS

Add the tuna fish can lid
    to the collection of serrated edges
    melted down to make new fillings,
just as the messenger is part
    of the message.
All dynasties eventually fade,
    but not before
    I obsessively check my email
    and automatic overdraft protection.

Thrift store trophies are handed out
    to the league's best carpet warmers
    at the end of the season.
I wiped up the sweat stain with a
    certificate for perfect attendance.
Otherwise, you can simply try to
    walk away or else burn it
    to the ground.
That's why I save string
    during rationing.

Stir the drink with a dirty finger—
    the whole shipment of Kool-Aid
    needs more flavor,
while millions of people
    have their homes taken away.

The next to go are the war reporters
     dumping unfinished mess-hall dinners
     into the trash.
Later on, it felt good to finally write
     that long letter.

SPEED IS FEASTING

The purse snatcher with a crooked wig
used the wrong stain lifter
on a collection of recycling bags
filled with the exaggerated minor details
of our eating habits and rhetorical versions
pushing cuticles past the knuckle.
That's strange, because I thought all I ever wanted
was words, as your language nets me
long before the contagious stage and its
what-have-you-done-for-me-lately?
measuring history from war to war.

Paranoia is looking in as the rates get raised,
not crazy for no reason, though we can do that too.
Like poetry, it's not a place for the proper.
It's not even a place,
but means getting beamed up by aliens
and put on juicer duty mixing
Christmas carols and codeine.
No wonder it sometimes seems as if
everything I learned is wrong,
yet there aren't any more lessons scheduled,
nothing but the recipe for turning
fungal infections into supplements.

That's because you might not know it's dead
until long after it's gone.
Besides, you don't just wake up one morning
and suddenly change your life.
I'm good at collecting shoes outside the prison
but not the names of supporting actors,
because if evil is personified,
it probably misses the larger systems
with their helicopters and seagulls
jostling for flyover rights,
and a dumpster's transparent tarp
blowing like a sail in our dreams.

The pillows were filled with grapes;
the bed was deeper than an ocean.
I can't believe I lived for a winter without heat.
The hospital is out of slings.
Better to show up anyway
and pretend you're a team player.
You can always pay someone to walk the dog
while you're staring out the window for hours
and never see anything green
except a weathered bronze memorial
to the survivors of a shipwreck
occurring right there in the harbor.

It's difficult to be a poet when you stop
receiving messages.
At work, I prefer to ease into my shift before
clearing the lunchroom where everybody
dislocated their shoulders, even on Sunday.
The sky is blue ahead of the storm.
A megaphone dangled from a streetlamp casting
as much shadow as light on a future
slumped over the wheel,
with a child's empty car seat in the back
and groceries spilling on the floor.

Can we talk about love now?
We take time back to the initial point of impact
while gagging on gerunds along the way.
I'm not sure we're ever going to make it home.
Fill the *river with sand.
Trucks drove emergency supplies in from an airport
seen on a series of receding screens
used to align shopping carts with dirty instruments
in the organ donors' dressing rooms.
A taste for the gamy troubles the kingdom
of plodding meats, even if
the processed is processed before we get to it.

* bower

SIGNAL CALLERS MEET THE WAVE MACHINE

SHED

We pay for the war regularly,
but it still won't go away,
along with an impulse to flicker
in time's radiance impossible to see.
At the kite festival there's always
more height than string.
I forget what I'm wearing
in the room next to dream.

But I wouldn't call them lies,
so I'll take more of everything
except musicals, veal,
and a nostalgia for whatever
doesn't fit, including terra cotta
statues lodged with this poem
in a mailroom sink leaned against
until the sun shines elliptical.

We perform circus tricks
on the couch with spinning plates
and loose change, because
the person with the most distractions
usually wins. The railyard's
noisy stutter hurts the animal
devices, its large steel couplers
squeezing the heart out of love.

HI, FIDELITY

I'm learning what the satellites teach me after they
rendered the wingdancers obsolete
along with their cracked piñata shower of hard candy
and toy soldiers

tying tourniquets improvised from treadmill belts.
Cartoon versions await our future,
our closets' stinging bee collections, put in the back
seat and driven with

the rest of our hearts into oncoming traffic stalled
in front of an aquarium supply store
and its grand opening featuring stabbed or grabbed
shrimp appetizers.

I'm found outside of me—a part of stars   classroom
cash register   a shovel patting soil
each with their posted menus of unzipped ribcages
and paper jams.

Earphones leak with digital bird songs and scheduled
bathroom-break spreadsheets.
But I'll never forget these quiet summer weeks with
you, resting

my head on the chest of the beefcake formerly known
as Valentine's Day, while outside,
leaves clap wildly in the wind. The theater is hosed
down after the movie's

done, like a bridge encrusted with wishes where
a car went over bumping fluorescent
lights strung from a dropped ceiling. I wish I could
unravel time

while sitting immobile during those moments
of dramatic change waving a knife
in my face, or maybe it was the drunks sunning
themselves in

the angular glow of light sabers, in the chance to
cook casseroles for children and
crows. You're right, there are very good reasons
to be either afraid

or fall asleep. Has the pet been fed? Sometimes
the only weapons are words during
a trip to the quarry with its mine-disaster machines
slowly scraping

along the edge of commands that some Americans
have for other Americans, a cracked
ruler drawing attention to chalkboard maps and
framed pictures

of kittens. You call it quality control; I call it
discarded, a broken-back smile
and nod that air-conditions fiberglass coffins tasting
like PlayStation

cartridges and the code for digital hardcore. Flies
bounce off the window, cracking
their black chandeliers spoken with a tongue previously
all teeth surrounded

by biographies and travel guides splitting infinitives
between them. High school students
intern at prisons. Talk show transcripts download
into a spam-ridden

inbox. Put the groceries on a credit card, and we'll
figure out how to pay for them later,
as well as the lawnmower and the local drugstore's
smells-like-a-

full-ashtray fragrance spray. No wonder I was always
nauseous while pregnant. I ate
a whole can of stewed tomatoes with a lead spoon.
The bartender

dropped by to wash the few dishes. Serving size
is irrelevant to take-out, because
belief isn't really the issue. Sophie knows both
love and monsters,

but can't see electricity. She doesn't understand
the concept of giving up. A garden
blooms fuller each year. Despite the subtle fingernail
tugging, nothing

else seems to matter, certainly not for the small
but active online community
of happy cat slappers. I looked up to see a river
flowing over

my head, then a nation's daguerreotypes archived
in a glass-bottomed boat. The brick
wall is painted a different color each year. Sheets
of paper drift against

a sky of blue valances striping bones like candy.
The stranger is a neighbor. Discount
stores close for the night, with its stretched signals,
its thinning beetles.

THE WAR AT HOME

We might suffer from allergies if there were any trees left,
but pollen still sticks to our hands and antennae, softened
and curled up before going to bed. I dreamt about bibimbap
on the menu. You know more songs. All that steel couldn't
secure the façade. We move a mountain one imaginary
spoonful at a time; we put it in the back of a U-Haul
for transport to the next tire shop, scrubbing tread marks
left in velvet shed from the antlers of dwindling herds.

Flyswatters double as spatulas at the State Fair pancake-
flipping contest. We choose between gas and food while
recording the radiologists' ecstatic visions. Just don't call it
news, and I'll get it wrong for as long as you want me to
or else imagine letting go of need, then do my best not
to mention a tourniquet. Cells have their own histories,
muscles twitch with electricity, like swallows darting from
a balcony at a thunderclap.

Every animal forgets its training—also known as the border
patrol. There's a different blade for cutting stone. We cover
the distance with soggy boots during tax season. My contribution
could easily fill a plastic cup or put more stories in a dictionary
written with cinnamon sticks mashed into eye shadow. Know
what I mean? Words bring the ghosts closer. There are plenty
of excuses for only eating icing, for replacing ant farm sand
with glitter.

The repairs are stopgap. For instance, I've never learned how
to make a viable paper airplane, and you're a perky sailor
who enjoys a post-workout smoke. The first thing I lost
was my mother's name; most recently, it was a lemon-scented
air freshener from the car wash. The sea shines through jellyfish
as the war stacks its dead next to gas stations, duct tape,
and Christmas lights wrapped around lawn sprinklers aimed
at a corner of the desert.

THE LOGIC OF DEFEAT

Me and the cashier grew up together.
    I've got a bundle of instant coupons
    clutched between my knees.
    Still, there's no starting over—
    just a series of unanticipated
    events, as the tow truck slips out
    of gear and rolls down the driveway
    into traffic. During summer months,
    the electricity runs for only a few
    hours per day. Everything green
    turned viscous and glistened.

If the fish rots from the head down,
    then that must be one enormous fish.
    Meanwhile, our mouths swell up
    with the taste of bee stings, and every
    lie is a confession. The rubbings made
    from gravestones were converted
    into postcards. My implant gives
    me an itchy rash, but I don't complain
    since it increases download speed,
    even if it means I can't eat eggs anymore.

Need more information. There are basic
    safety precautions to be taken
    with plastics and everyday lawn care
    that don't involve a long-term

past. Or a truncated future.
It's also how I ended up living
in the guestroom feeding shredded
mailing labels to mechanical tarantulas
in an opaque vase.

Night slowly creeps across the TV screen,
    like a Ferris wheel pulling the covers
    over its head while furtively listening
    to reports on infrastructure after
    a disaster has happened. It's not
    about us anymore, although I'm
    just short of professional. It's the
    hour when people tend to be sleeping,
    anti-static lip gloss applied
    for the astral commute.

( )

Most of the zoo animals
were oblivious to their viewers
despite the sweaty hands
and faces leaning into their
cages. Impulse control only
gets one so far. Passenger
planes swerve to avoid
bomb craters pockmarking
a runway and its sliver
of bone persistently lodged
in the throat. It's congenital
and yet too busy to remember,
spooning thickened sediment
from a muddy puddle.

While letting go means
it might never come back
or maybe it will in a different
form, it's hard to be Zen
about the smell of fried
bacon that won't wash out
of these waitressing clothes.
There's no such thing
as a permanent circus,
especially when the rodeo
clowns stop buying tickets.
Sometimes, being completely
literal confuses the system.
These new swivelless barstools
are starting to grow on me;
next up are replacement gums
in beta testing.

It's okay to get your hopes
up, but just remember that
the law packs its own lunch
for the office. Plunging
necklines briefly confuse
the guillotinists, their blunt
edge bouncing off the tweener
scoreboard, as some receive
justice and others endure it.
The rest was left to Ambien
know-how and air guitar
contestants feigning surprise
when groupies grope the
soundman during the "Stairway
to Heaven" solo practiced
in front of a bathroom mirror.

Lost in space sold us on
the arrangement. I rarely
remember my dreams, except
for the one about the ashram
I'd visited with my ex-wife
being demolished to make
room for a hospital, and
the Mexican restaurant
subsequently forced to move
down the street; oh, yeah,
and there was an imaginary
map of India that doubled
as a kid's ghost costume
I showed to a co-worker
while riding on a train.

Squeeze the toy bird's chest
if you want to hear it chirp.
A helicopter sweeps burning
cars and dairy farms with
a searchlight flashing rectangles
on the carpet that look like
a child's blocky letter version
of Morse code spelling P-E-A-C-E.
I just want a little bit of peace.
The next morning the dishes
were still piled up in the sink.
That's when I remembered
your tip for getting a pedicure—
it involves clean dress socks
and open sores. Sorry, I meant
to say sinecure.

That's right about the time
when the line went dead,
with fingers curled tight
around the receiver and stitches
pulling out with the removed
masking tape. Most enemies
are imagined, but not the nest
sagging down to the snake.
So good riddance to all that
`history purring with arched
back and rubbing against our
knees, as the bass rumbles
low inside cars double-parked
in front of the cake shop.

SHOOT A KITE

Even with the hall light
switched on,
we still stumble down
the basement's
narrow set of stairs.
A complex consists
of passages and shelters
carpeted to discharge
its blue electric memory.
In a discontinued model
of a popular family sedan,
Pepsi and hair gel blow
through the air vents
and onto our tan pantsuits
blending with the upholstery
torn on the shred
of a posted eviction notice.
It's the epoch of lots
of plastic straws,
of digital printing.
No information is bad,
as the media eats the media
in the leaked-before-
the-release-date version
of burying our faces
in the produce aisle display,
minus art and carbohydrates,

which make my
blood sugar glisten.
I'm not afraid
of the ghosts I see,
only the ones I don't,
because eyes
are the first tombs,
quoting the whiff
of another fragrance
in chiseled sans serif.
But it was an absurd moment
to be masticating paper hats
and wearing sequined chaps
after all the food
in the refrigerator
rotted during the blackout.

STAIN GUARD

Vast cloud formations push through
during the course of the afternoon,
much to the deaf window washers'
signed delight. Back inside,
there's an art to alienating your
bridge partner, especially the one
doing all the heavy lifting. Me?
No, I'm still gathering shards
and researching moving boxes online.

I'm an absent father to an absent son
at the tail end of the age of mammals
inhaling jet fumes. I spent any money
I made later that same day.
It takes a goat whisperer to coax
the damaged ones back into the pen.
Power lines droop with wet spring snow,
fitting a couple more letters
on the outside of an envelope.

It's the global-trade-routes sound,
the searchlight that never illuminates
the underside of leaves and their chewed
fingerprints dressing the wounds
left by the sharp-edged pleats
of imperial curtsies. At best,
the accommodations were temporary;

at worst, permanent—waking up
the next day to sleepily shuffle
through the breakfast buffet line.

Like an immense pack of invisible
blue lions, nature separates and kills.
A modem's light blinks its feeding,
while we never eat at home
but instead strip the battlefield
of fatigues and change the night-sweat
sheets. My dreams tend to be literal.
We make mirrors from sputtering
flyovers clustering cache data,
or invent an elaborate plot device
to bring a dead TV character back to life.

STATIC HAT

(Last night I almost pulled in the signal of a house burning in the distance.)

(Closer is just as far from there.)

(The package never got delivered.)

(When you smile that way it fills me with light.)

(Why should everyone be required to speak English?)

(I decided to invent the hot air balloon.)

(Poetry is like a mouthwash siphon.)

(Clowns can seem frightening to children.)

(We left select answers blank on the aptitude test.)

FOR
FUTURE
TRIPS
OR
EVERYDAY
LIFE

INTERIOR DESIGN

At this point, I don't remember what we were fighting
about, although I think it had something to do with
the inverse of our desires and impairment, which may
help explain my recurring dream of a windowless van
for changing into a hand-crocheted superhero outfit
that shrank in the head and arm regions after repeated
washings meant to get out the more conspicuous stains.

Perhaps not uncoincidentally, that's what it's like
at home, with the aging family dog no longer able to
distinguish between a piece of leftover steak and the hand
proffering it, which isn't the same as ubiquitous pawing,
with its tensions of legibility wearing the kitty down
to a nub. It's also where the police go for their double lattes.

In other words, I'm more than happy to skirt the authority
of false authorities with their refugee-camp tourism.
And if you want to reach me during the next couple hours,
I'll be back at the laundromat—the one by the Taco Bell
and Dairy Queen. Afterward, I walked to the gas station
to get a pack of cigarettes while you ate pork chops
with maple syrup. It was dusk. We weren't fighting.

EVERY ONCE IN A WHILE I AM PERMITTED

Just like in the kids' film, developers bulldoze
a meadow where we imagined playing,

                              while shell casings

drop on charcoal maps and seduce our collection
of glue sticks. It's now and never.

                              I sometimes smoke

because it makes me feel lighter, so just be glad
I'm not famous. Splayed clouds

                              frame a wall

framing a sky, as my hands shake a viewfinder
tracking an early winter sun

                              setting in a hurry.

Thanks, Mom. I love language. I'm pumped up
on supplements, scripted with software,

                              and up to my elbows

in bones. I turn off all the lights before leaving
the house, and sometimes without

                                   leaving the house,

because proper behaviors are played like a game.
But I still want to make things

                                   and change things.

I still like to see power disgraced. It's not irony;
it's ruin. Even astronauts put

                                   their boots up

at the orthodontist where little lasers whiten
teeth and zap empty Budweiser cans

                                   floating in orbit.

From earth, it all looked like shimmying piles
of Vaseline in a facility processing

                                   mostly nuts and dry skin.

MEANS TO AN END

We tell winter our names
and protect our heads while sleeping
but not the get-well-soon cards
knocked off TV trays bent into mirrors
slippery with beer and smashed
against an oar's splintered remains
as children thrust their arms
into a pharmacy's decorative wishing well.

There are homes you will never see again,
which has only partly to do
with the present state of architecture
organizing the space between dog and leash—
the width of an angel's wing—
walked in a park commemorating
the polar expedition member
who refused to get out of bed before noon.

Helicopter blades slice off treetops
we wear as hats for the rest of the fashion season
even after the judge requested
we remove them in the courtroom
to the sound of nervous laughter
and the snap of unfastened holsters
worn by amateur magicians exiting
toward the fog machines.

I know I've made mistakes,
but there's no such thing as a confession,
only a different portrait painted
for each sitter turning green
from the overseasoned meat.
I'll be in the kitchen washing the dishes
and watching butterflies migrate
along a flyway lined with McDonald's signs
adding verbs to an obstacle course.

The first dream was about loss;
the second was about finding directions.
Nurses on a smoking break huddle
together outside in the cold after a shift
spent tending to ripped-out piercings;
ambulances shake curbside
with their heaters on high
warming bags of plasma and needles
coughed on by the words for divorce.

—Winter 2007

TRANSDERMAL EXPRESS

1)

Even terrariums
aren't exempt
from the renaming
process accompanying
the project for a new
American century.
The show features
hourly winners with
hotel accommodations
provided by a fleet
of sunken tuna boats
that once housed
the homeless beneath
constellations beamed
at low ceilings by
desktop planetariums.
No wonder the butcher
is an insomniac,
because if it becomes
too painful, can it
still be called irony?

2)

What do The Fonz
and Eazy-E have
in common?
This is the mixtape
version of the mixtape
version, splitting history
into parallax, because
there's no big picture,
only lots of small ones
on screens in various
configurations, like
beauty salon software
previewing hairstyles
for a fee. So bring
a passport or Green Card
photo, but don't eat
the plastic cashews.
They're purely decorative,
and like cold weather
slow down the relentless
roaches, though not
the creditors seeking
payment for the harnesses
and aprons dispensed
alongside soft-serve
ice cream machines.

3)

During an anachronistic
historical reenactment
I stuffed the musket
with lead, cotton batting,
gunpowder, more lead,
more cotton batting,
mayonnaise, crumpled
parking tickets,
a fruity cocktail's
miniature pink umbrella,
and a disposable
eye patch—then
immediately discharged it
in the direction of a
grey-uniformed doctor,
because for a moment
I lost track of my
time zone along with
migrating geese,
the partially unwitting stars
of *Girls Gone Wild, Vol. 4,*
and a man in a gorilla suit
unintentionally scaring
children at a birthday
party. Yes, I know this
is all going to come back
to haunt me during
any potential future run
for public office.

4)

Sailors, surfers,
and swimmers
use a mechanical
shark's fin as a
makeshift sundial,
forgetting the
accumulating late
fees on land paid
in meatloaf slices
stuffed with small
rubber bands.
Something living
once inhabited
that shell. Similarly,
you'd think the
neighbor's dog
would be hoarse
from all that barking
into a house with
its crime-scene
investigators dressed
in rags and its speed
monitored by
low-flying aircraft.

5)

A gas station's bright
Exxon sign illuminates
a living room.
Transgression may be
an attempt to get at
the real, but what if
the real can't be got
at? It's a long wait
for the bus. They didn't
remove my lung;
they only moved it.
So how much do I owe
the compensating ghosts
charging for both
bruise and poultice,
for each week split
into sharp angles,
and a desert given
the choice of being
consumed by itself,
an army, or a water park?

6)

We change out of
dirty clothes into
dirtier clothes to watch
desire fall in love
with its dumbwaiter,
a double-jointed
equinox warming
the garage but keeping
the kitchen cold,
or a website's rapidly
rotating headlines featuring
a donkey tugging
on a fallen clown's
jaw mumbling about
a kinder and gentler
vacation, because I too
once dreamed of
saving the world;
now I'm trying
to prepare it
for my daughter
and other imagined
communities, while
the rules for writing
change all the time—
trading in an opaque
currency.

7)

First the architecture
then the night begins
to breathe through us.
There's an exciting
array of choices
when it comes to
face, hand, and body
moisturizers. A small
brushfire broke out
in the next aisle over.
Clerks calmly alerted
the manager and
returned to their registers.
Afterward, I couldn't
get the car to slow
down until it hit
a row of trash cans
spilling buckets
of fake snow and old
answering machine
recordings. Anything
to get me away
from here, because
anticipating the disaster
can sometimes be worse
than experiencing it,

like a series of
overcompensations
a human cannonball
makes in order to hit
a receding target.

NERVOUS CONDITIONS

The state property yard sale takes place outside
the barbed wire this year, though the warden
usually reserves the best artwork for the nightshift
and its Payless synthetic leather, its briefcase
resembling a goth girl's skull-shaped purse cradling
a clanking keychain. That's why it's never silent
in the library where everything's untrue except
for a respite from the loud barking interrupting
conjugal visits.

No matter. There's always the converted cement
mixer discharging massive sno cones melting
all over our torsos speckled with leftover wedding
cake stains that fade like carnival game tickets
accidentally going through the wash in a pant's pocket.
So what else besides medical waste should we stick
in this garbage bag before it gets put out in the morning?
And how did we end up throwing away all the stuff
we don't need except for need itself?

Robots do a shoddy job making sweetheart bracelets
from dried macaroni, diamonds, and string,
since whatever's edible confuses them, while we
eat chips and barcodes. The first things I'll do
are request a neck transplant and order a separate
room for the mosquitoes we seem to have taken

with us on a vacation mostly spent poolside
washing down muscle relaxants with piña coladas
before noon.

A blimp briefly blotted out the sun then the moon,
as part of the crowd cheered and part of it slept.
It costs almost an arm to fill up the car for driving
around in circles or for another trip to the vet where
the spinal adjustments are cheaper, the chew toys
more durable, and the personal ads mixed species,
even if sometimes we're broke on purpose.
I love recovering the scattered bits of Osiris—
I could be his mother.

There are lots of reasons for staying close
to the floor while the turrets swivel in circles,
ripping badminton nets from their flimsy base
and making sure the debris is saved for cineplex
seating. Okay, roll credits, but don't infantilize me.
It's hard enough to get taken seriously by
the protocolers shouting, "Stand up straight!"
as if there's a vast conspiracy hatching to rob them
of their land.

The cold sweats became this summer's dance craze
turning small walk-on parts into run-ons and
hosting casting calls for giraffes under lowered
power lines. There's no time off for good behavior,

no outselling a fading celebrity's motivational tape,
while afternoon clouds roll in without an adjective.
But we like to talk on the phone late at night,
the yeses and nos more permeable popping
a language that blurs sound and noise.

THE FIRST LINE OF THIS POEM IS

the first line of this poem
spinning a pith helmet
missing its chin strap
the distant hum of freeway
traffic lulls the land
of the lost to sleep
along with the metaphors
blinking in an orange
roadside sign emptied
of meal tickets
then there was the time
I fainted while waiting
for the toxicology reports
to come back less than
thorough

A graveyard of TV screens
beep-beeps a metal detector
scanning paving stones
for the beach as chubby
chasers distractedly chat up
the attenuated at a party
Nixon's drunk again
a bar of soap melted
in the puddle of itself
we rationed for washing
our hands and the cat

but not the ironing board
a birthing shark ripped a
chunk out of after surfacing
through the floor

Still it cuts both ways
because it's better to bite
the shark than jump it
gold lamé is the new sun
in a playground behind
the dream of spring
as the radio loses its
volume in a confession
booth soundproofed with
a salted bone bruise sold
at a dollar store known
for its unique approach
to keeping meat cold
through the extended
holiday season

The wounded protect
the damaged when they're
not inflicting it themselves
thinking we got here on
our own while ignoring
the nearby ushers pointing
to the empty seats and

complimentary needles
we lick the loose threads
and sprinkle them with
glitter because waiting
is the moment most waited
for using a frayed towel
to blot the honeycomb's
sticky crust

AN ARCHITECTURE

Then there are the ones who go missing, the ones left incomplete. I know the whole fucking system is compromised. For the caption to our faux Wild West sepia-toned portrait, you chose Booty Bandit for your outlaw alias. I momentarily forgot that One-Armed Bandit means a slot machine, so instead settled for Clementine-Who-Spent-Years-Trying-to-Get-the-Toilet-Out-of-the Kitchen.

A symptom defines its truth; reality is a symptom opening doors and windows to a night spreading low over the kingdom, hidden fingers interlaced with a glacier. Tens of billions more will be spent on the war, not including the secret programs. I don't want to play Penelope to your Ulysses, or Ulysses to your Penelope, because once you enter a particular stretch of desert, the signs say no services for miles.

Sometimes home isn't any cozier with its history of dismantlement measured in layers of linoleum and annual 4th of July parties, while children take cover beneath the bleachers. The small-town Air & Space Museum stayed open late, since it still felt warm to the touch, as the resistance of veterans comes to grief. You shouldn't have to pay to boo on free beer night after watching the highlights.

MAN IN THE MIRROR

Shooting stars bounce off a biodome's steel frame
enclosing viruses and practical open-toe footwear,
while discount shoppers alphabetize the various
additives in Hershey's syrup with a lung condition.
The caption for a photo of José Padilla read,
"Location unknown, not dated," as the dead
wear ghosts for clothes in burial's closed circuitry
losing the person for the personal. Where, then,
do pearls come from?—from the clogged tear ducts
of roadkill scurrying into increased bandwidth
for birdwatchers given binoculars and smog.

Contrary to what gets edited, I've tried to fix it.
So why am I doing this isn't such an illogical
question, because your poems haven't won me—
they gum me. There's a massive international
black market for baby formula and whatever else
is in that plastic bottle, such as quality time with
a cologne daubed on sagging botoxed wattles.
Let's argue about money again in an archive
of wedding photos squinted at through thick-lens
glasses placed in a box covered with enough stamps
for mailing they obscured most of the address.

SIGN OF THE TIMES (WITH PRINCE
AND THE SPACEAPE IN MIND)

Hollowed-out bones are more buoyant,

like the stray dog wagging its tail

while following us back to the car.

You asked if we could keep it;

I said that whatever gets buried

eventually climbs out of its hole,

and just because something can float

doesn't mean it can swim.

So I'll hold this snackpack close to my chest

as we head toward open water, especially

now that meals have been discontinued

on most long-distance flights,

but people still want to fly.

THE SERVICE ECONOMY'S ECONOMY

A vacant lot is the playground where
    hungry ghosts prepare their meals
    using discarded microwaves and watery
    wine cooler bottle shards.
Wow, that's a big toxic spill.
Some mammals escape through the office building's
    rotating doors; others squeeze through
        the bulletproof portholes.

The bank still won't cash my check
    from the street fair's inflatable carousel
    after we ate with our elbows and assisted
    the blowtorches and spring planting.
Otherwise, it's gymnastics
    with knees firmly stuck to the petroleum floor
    while pretending to elude the chalk-outline
        authorities.

The surveillance cameras record without words,
    so we tried to confuse them with the scratch'n'sniff.
What's wrong with a little bit of good daddy?
This poem is like a birdcall
    that also attracts the cat,
    as some pain never gets taken away,
    but instead slips in its orbit—
        same hammer, different nail.

All my loves are outside the door,
    but all that history comes inside.
I get restless with feeling restless,
    and occasionally apologize for wanting more.
Welcome to the big anti-,
    to endless rows of binary code, to the difference
    between chicken fingers and feather fingers,
        and a bake sale held to help elect a new president.

Wait, wait, I'm not done yet.
The image-shades pursue us
    while hiding the somnambulists' map behind
    everything lost or damaged in the move.
The collar stretches from here to D.C.,
    though the dog hair is our own where the machines
    chomp down with mostly molars and we grab at
        serrated knife points combing the warm sand.

Sometimes we learn last,
    as wind and waves blow off the East River
    for another summer and wrap us in red curtains
    during musical chairs without sound or seating.
In a previous life, I was reincarnated
    as Long Island.
Forests intrude on our ears—
    the organ slowest to acknowledge goodbye.

A blanket of plastic pinwheels spins in the night,
  but we breathe so quietly beneath it
  when we're at peace.
It's the house that best fits our back
  on a street lined with aluminum siding
  because I'm not nostalgic for much of anything
  except the future and maybe that smudge
    you left on the sun.

This book was set in Bruce Old Style. The digital version used to set this book was created by Bitstream after a metal typeface designed by Sol Hess in 1909, after the New York-based Bruce Type Foundry's typeface, Old Style No. 20, created in 1869.

This first edition, first printing includes 26 limited edition copies lettered A-Z and signed by the author.